Romance

for Bassoon and Piano

Edward Elgar

OPUS 62

ISBN: 978-0-8536-0440-2

NOVELLO
part of **WiseMusic**Group

EXCLUSIVELY DISTRIBUTED BY

Visit Hal Leonard Online at
www.halleonard.com

Contact us:
Hal Leonard
7777 West Bluemound Road
Milwaukee, WI 53213
Email: info@halleonard.com

In Europe, contact:
Hal Leonard Europe Limited
42 Wigmore Street
Marylebone, London, W1U 2RY
Email: info@halleonardeurope.com

In Australia, contact:
Hal Leonard Australia Pty. Ltd.
4 Lentara Court
Cheltenham, Victoria, 3192 Australia
Email: info@halleonard.com.au

ROMANCE.

Edward Elgar, Op. 62.

Bassoon.

PIANO.

To Mr. Edwin F. James.

ROMANCE.

Edward Elgar, Op. 62.

13193
Copyright, 1910, by Novello & Company, Limited.

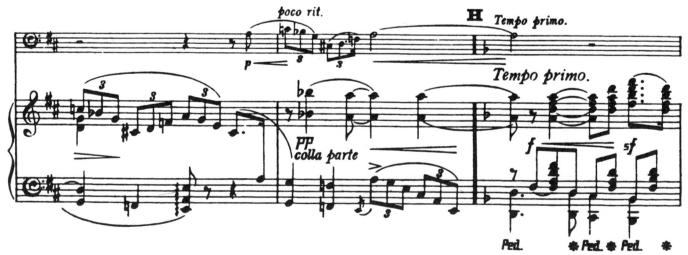

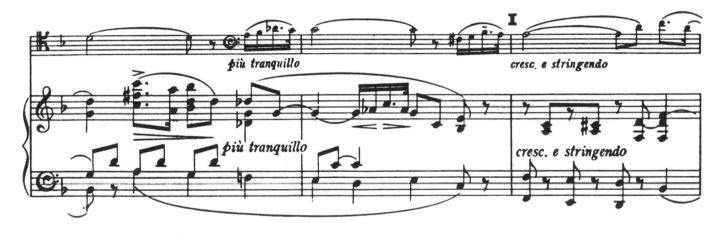